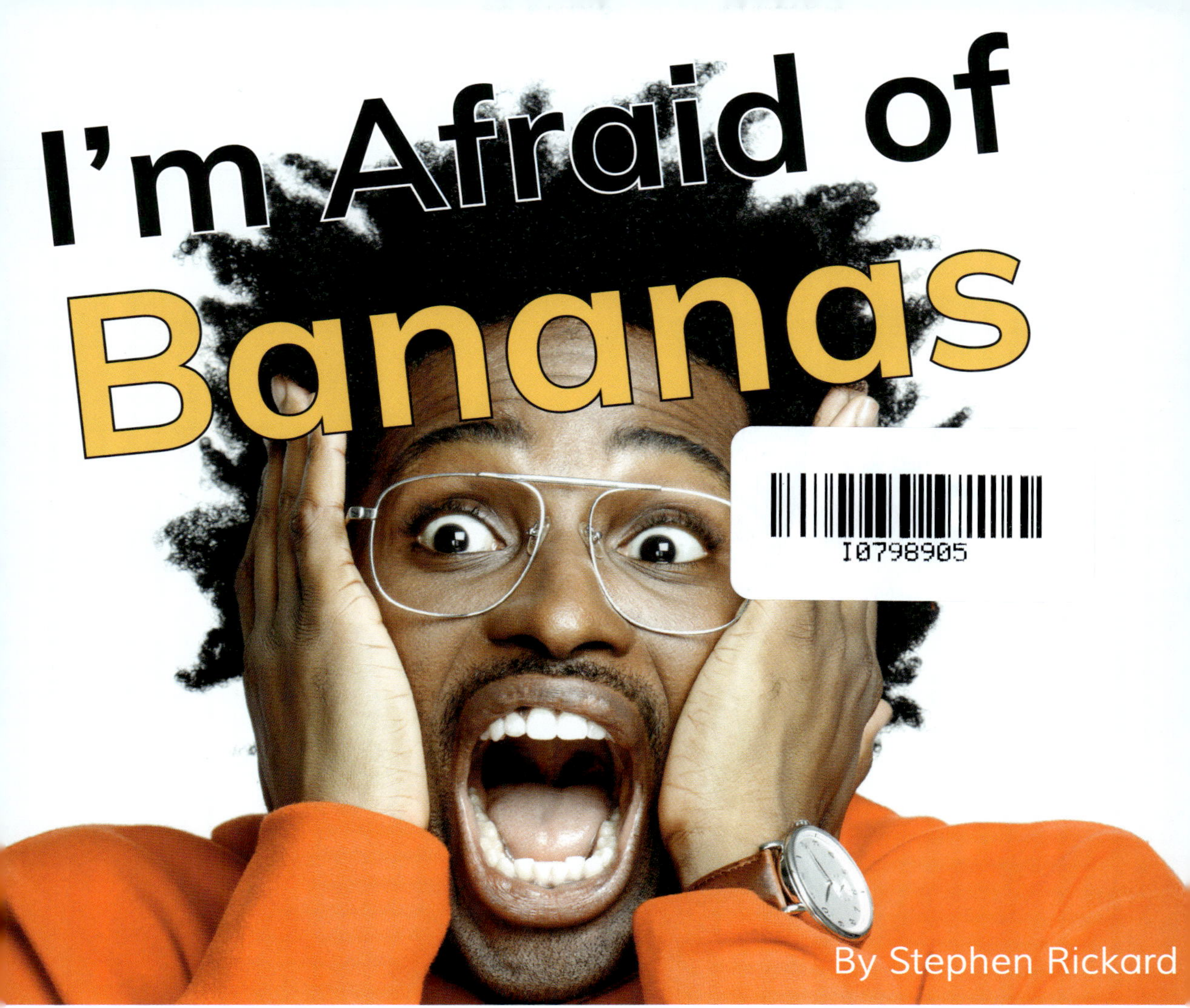

I'm Afraid of Bananas

By Stephen Rickard

Published in 2026 by
Norwood House Press
2544 Clinton Street
Buffalo, NY 14224

Printed in the United States of America

Library of Congress Cataloging-in-Publication Data:
Names: Rickard, Stephen, 1957-, author.
Title: I'm afraid of bananas ; The creature with nine brains / Stephen Rickard.
Description: Buffalo, NY : Norwood House Press, 2026. | Series: Phonics all-stars: phase 5c
Identifiers: ISBN 9781978578326 (pbk.) | ISBN 9781978578333 (library bound) | ISBN 9781978578340 (ebook)
Subjects: LCSH: Reading–Phonetic method–Juvenile literature. | English language–Phonetics–Juvenile literature. | Phobias–Juvenile literature. | Fear–Juvenile literature. | Octopuses–Juvenile literature.
Classification: LCC LB1573.3 R534 2026 | DDC 372.465–dc23

CPSIA compliance information: Batch #CW26NHP: For further information contact Norwood House Press at 1-800-237-9932.

Little kids are often scared of the dark, or of monsters under the bed.

Many grown-ups are afraid of things like crocodiles, bears, or thunderstorms.

Some people have a fear of things that might not seem frightening to us.

Do you have friends who are afraid of snakes or spiders? You might think that spiders aren't creepy, but you might understand why some people are frightened of them.

This might seem odd or funny, but some people have a fear of bananas.

For these people, this is no joke. It can make life very challenging for them.

There is one lady who is so afraid of bananas that she cannot see one, or smell one, without panicking and feeling very ill.

If she enters a room where a banana has been – even if it's not there now – she can still smell it.

That makes her feel very sick.

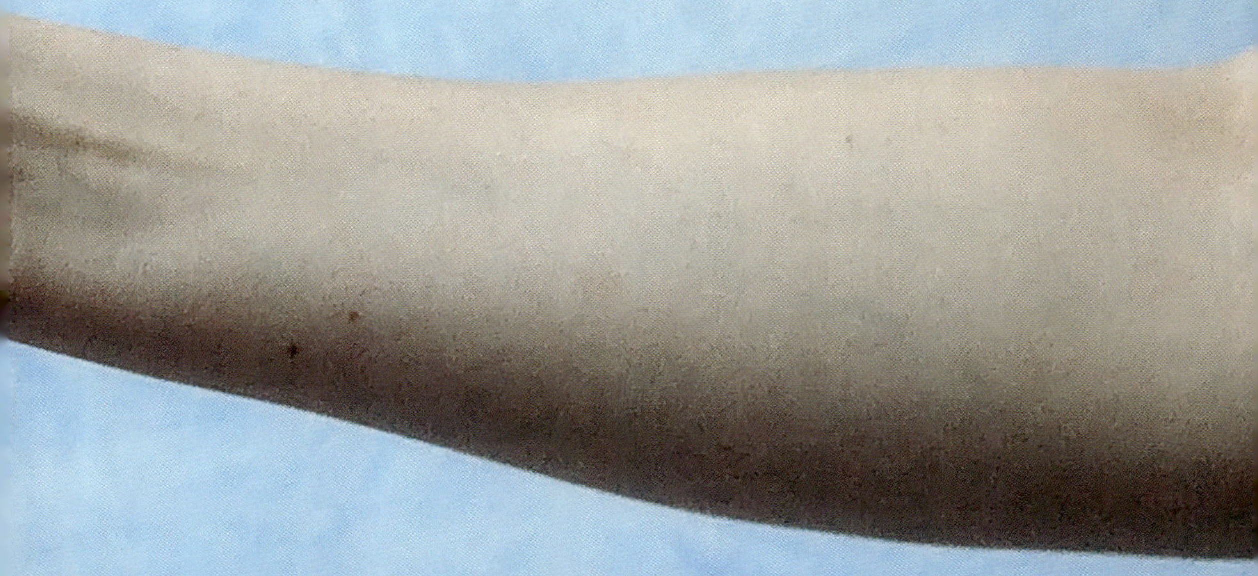

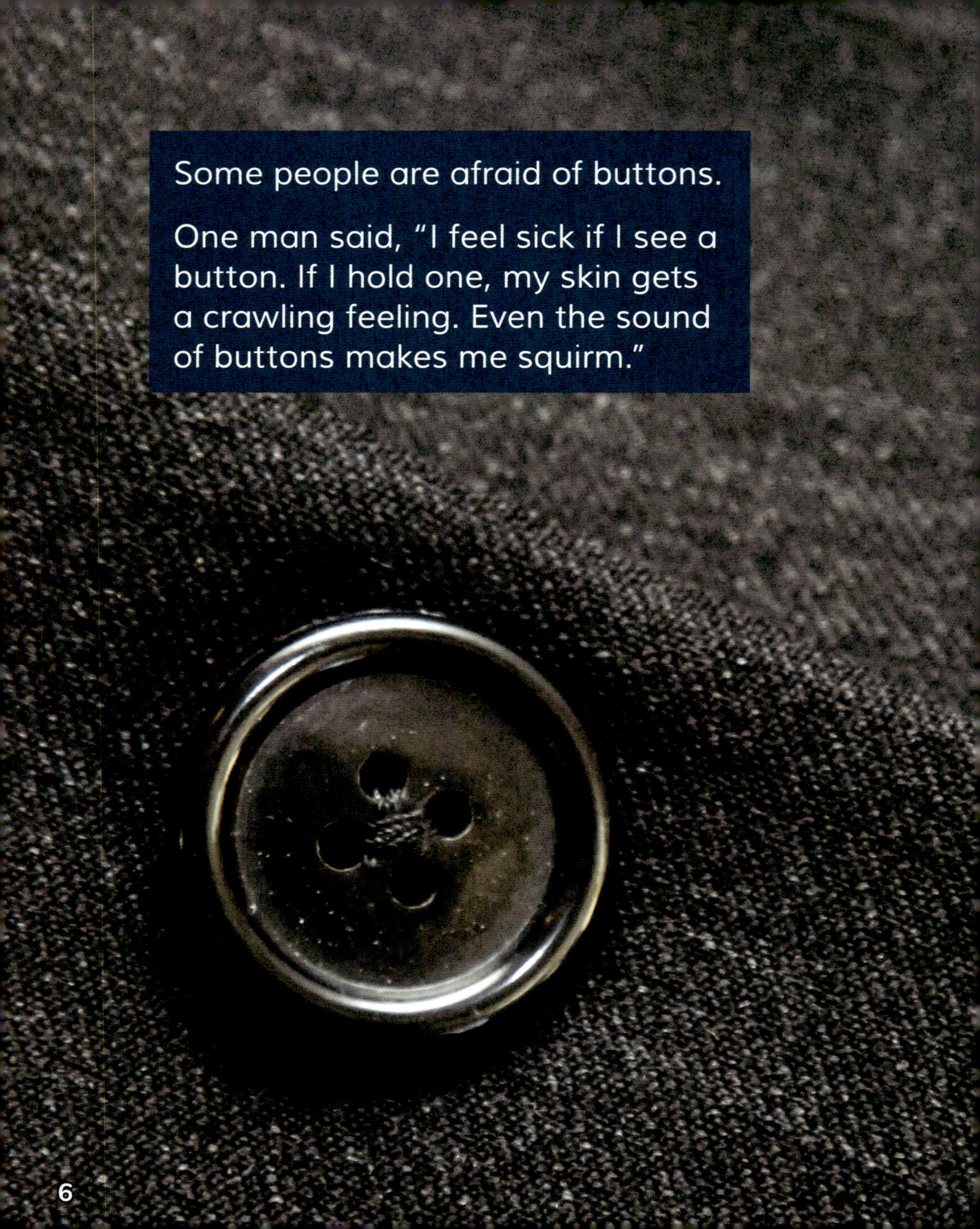

Some people are afraid of buttons.

One man said, “I feel sick if I see a button. If I hold one, my skin gets a crawling feeling. Even the sound of buttons makes me squirm.”

He cannot even have buttons on his clothes. For him, shopping for clothes must be tricky.

Other things people have a fear of include:

- balloons
- grass
- money
- numbers
- mirrors

Here are four more:

- small rooms or spaces
- yellow things
- clowns
- string

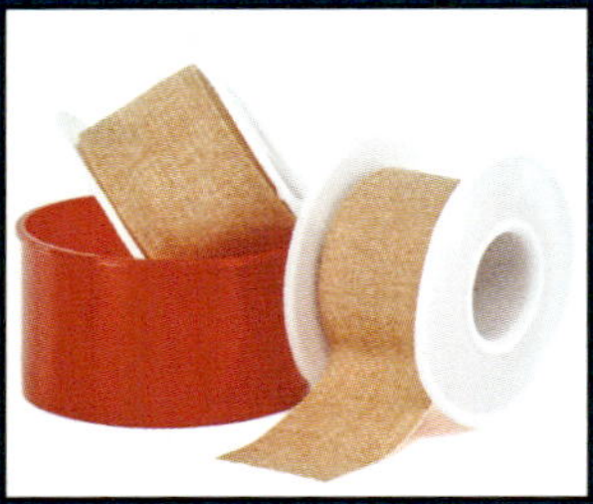

One of the oddest fears is a fear of belly buttons. People with this fear have to stick tape over their own belly button to hide it.

Another odd fear is a fear of peanut butter sticking to the roof of your mouth.

This might all seem very amusing, but for the people with these fears it can be a major problem.

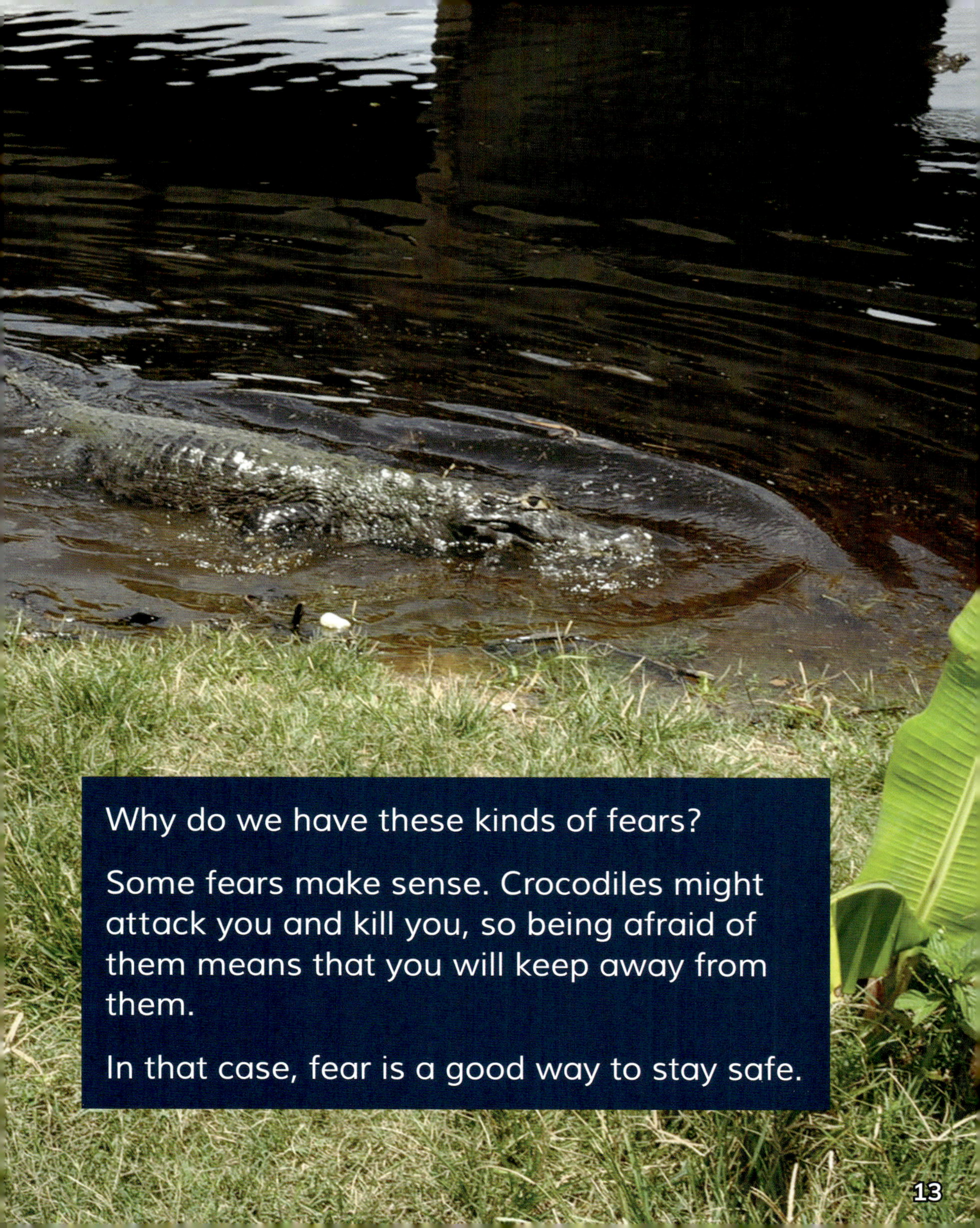

Why do we have these kinds of fears?

Some fears make sense. Crocodiles might attack you and kill you, so being afraid of them means that you will keep away from them.

In that case, fear is a good way to stay safe.

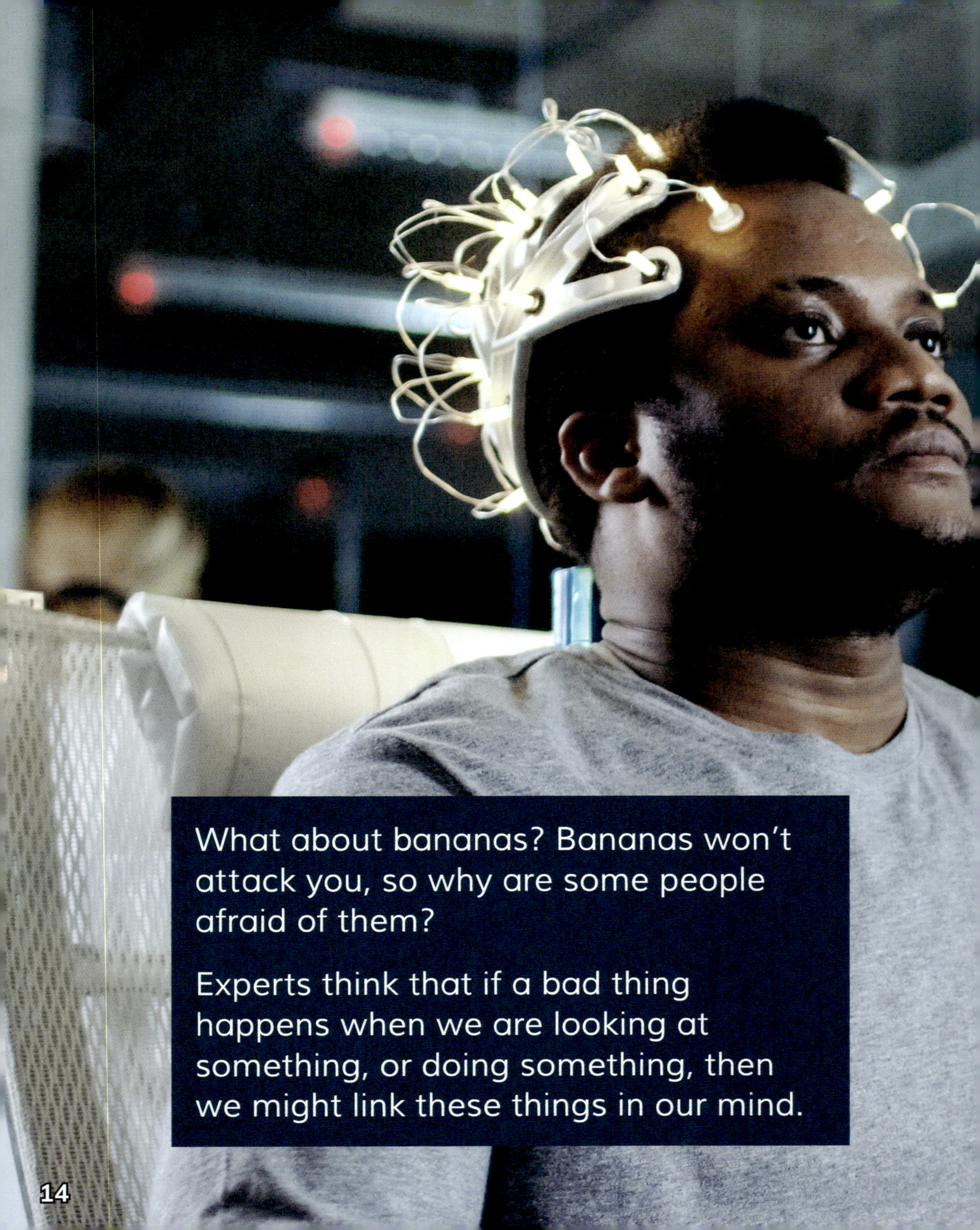

What about bananas? Bananas won't attack you, so why are some people afraid of them?

Experts think that if a bad thing happens when we are looking at something, or doing something, then we might link these things in our mind.

One girl had a big electric shock as a child, and she was looking at a bowl of bananas when she got the shock. This "taught" her mind that the bananas had something to do with it.

After that, whenever she saw or smelled bananas, her body reacted strongly: "Get away! These bananas mean danger."

Now, what are your fears? Do you have any?

The Creature with Nine Brains

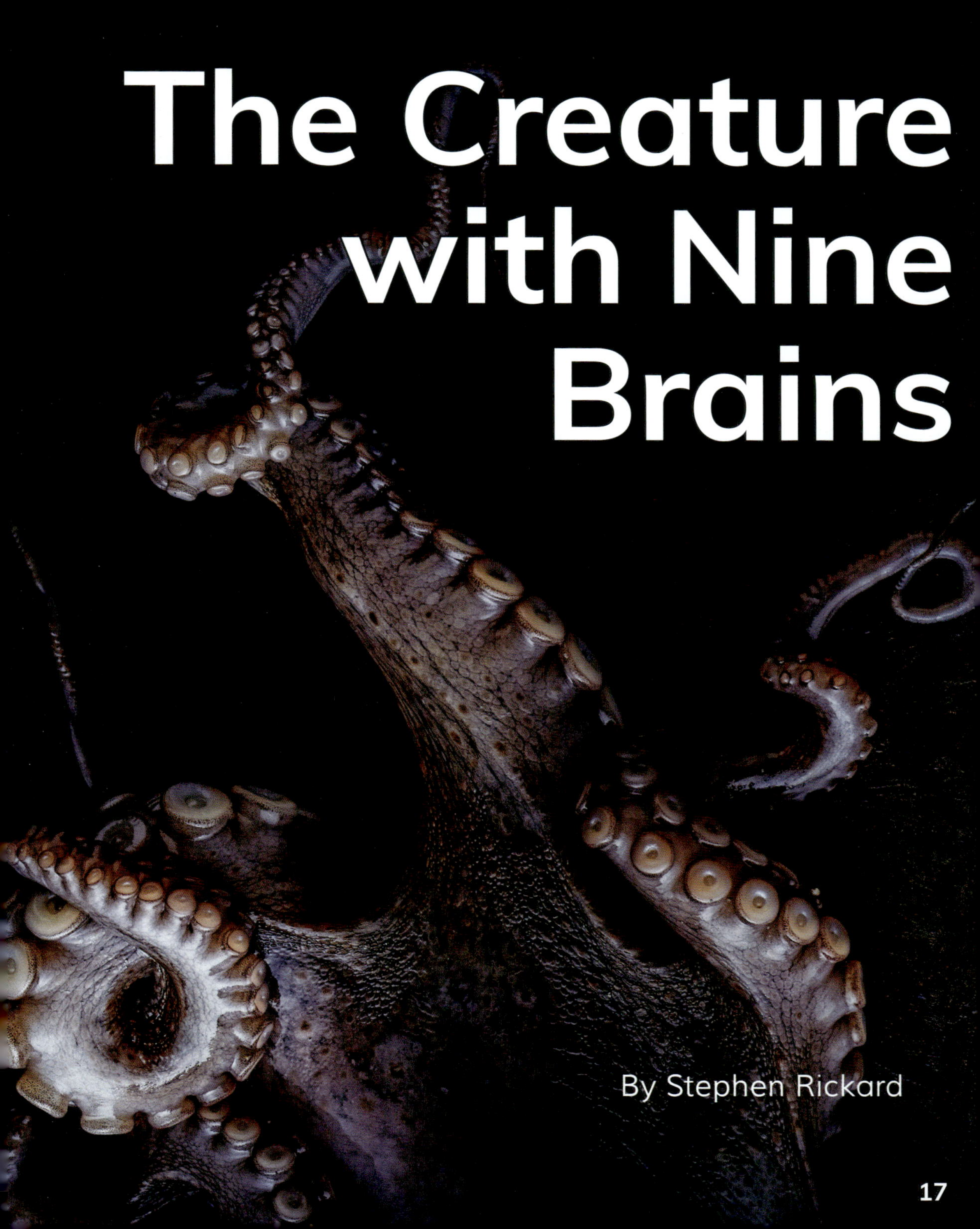

By Stephen Rickard

All animals on planet earth are part of a bigger family.

So cats belong to a family of animals that includes tigers and lions. Dogs are related to foxes.

Have you ever thought about the humble octopus?

This is such an odd creature in so many ways.

A cuttlefish

A squid

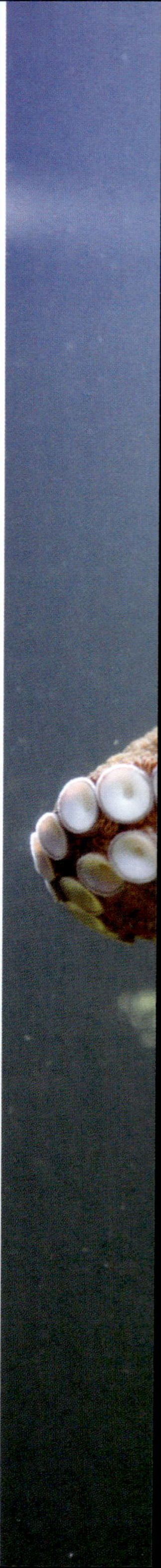

An octopus

Octopuses belong to a family that includes squid and cuttlefish.

However, they are much stranger than any of those creatures.

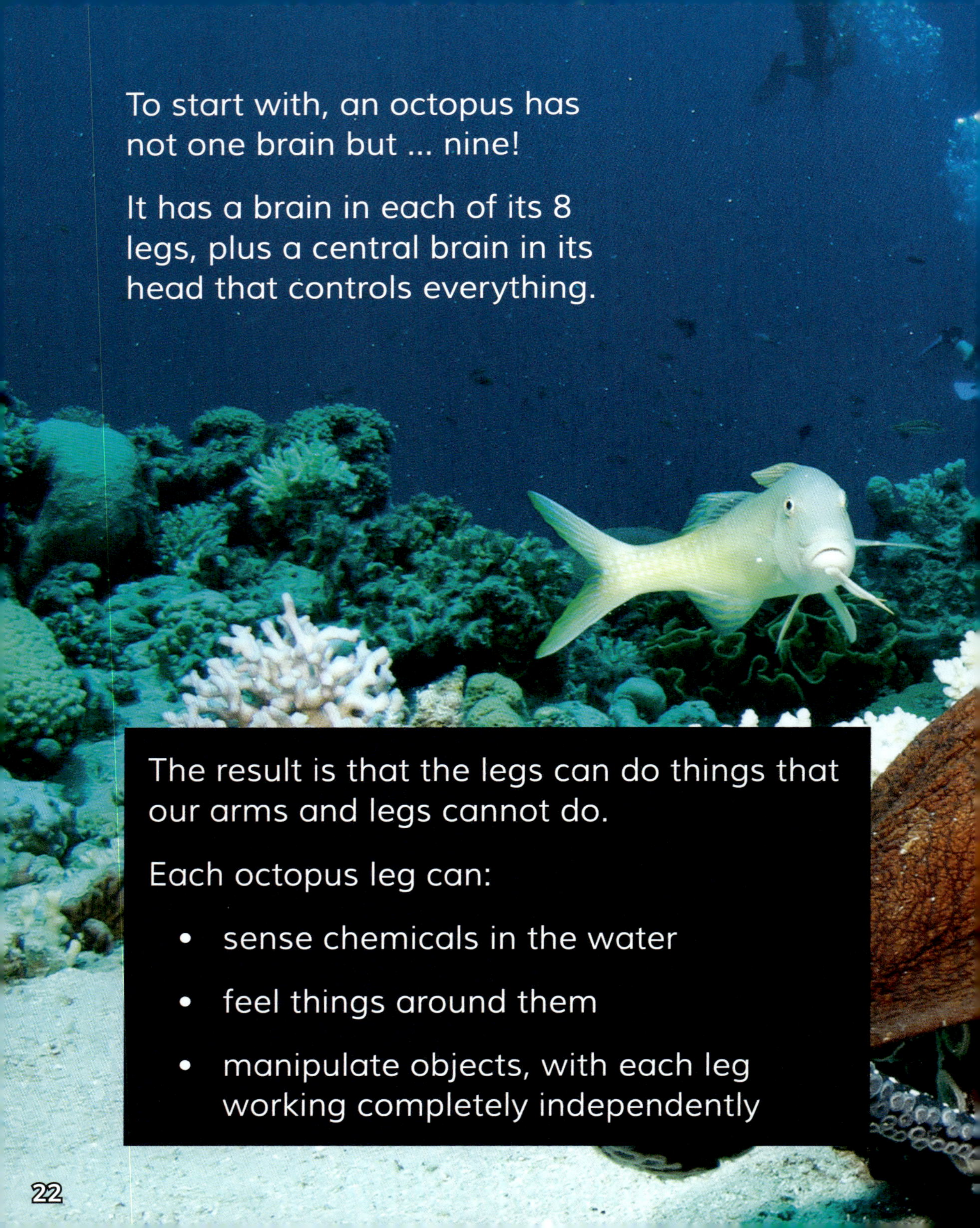

To start with, an octopus has not one brain but ... nine!

It has a brain in each of its 8 legs, plus a central brain in its head that controls everything.

The result is that the legs can do things that our arms and legs cannot do.

Each octopus leg can:

- sense chemicals in the water
- feel things around them
- manipulate objects, with each leg working completely independently

Each leg can sense and respond to light as well. So an octopus can "see" the world, even if its eyes are covered up.

That's quite incredible!

An octopus can blend in with its background too, by changing its skin from, say, red to blue.

The **mimic octopus** has to be the most impressive. It can transform its body so that it looks like a completely different animal.

It impersonates animals that other predators tend to avoid, which helps to protect it.

This mimic octopus is pretending to be a flounder.

Octopuses are highly intelligent, despite the fact that they learn nothing from their mom and dad, and must pick things up as they go through life.

They like to investigate their surroundings, as you can see in this picture.

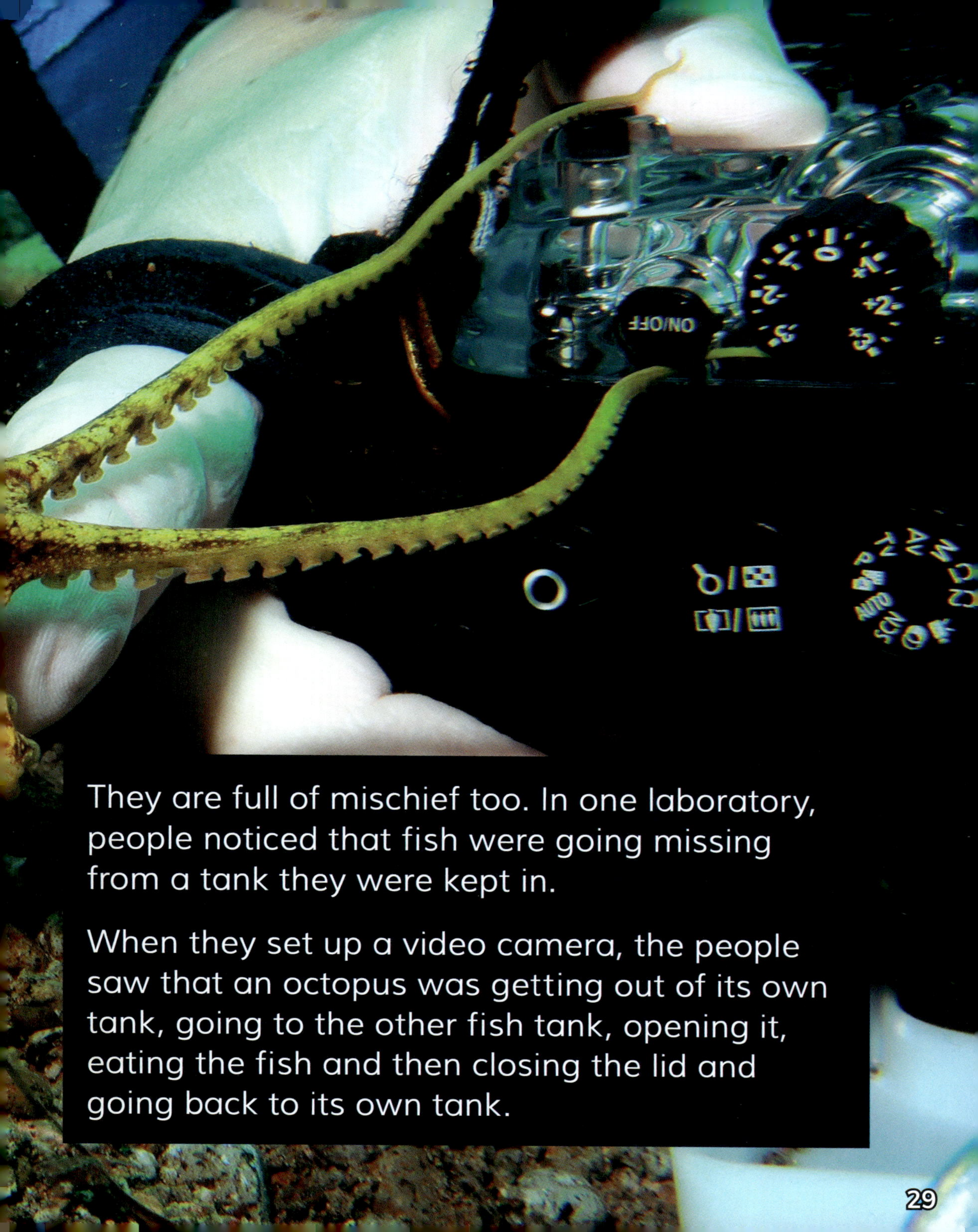

They are full of mischief too. In one laboratory, people noticed that fish were going missing from a tank they were kept in.

When they set up a video camera, the people saw that an octopus was getting out of its own tank, going to the other fish tank, opening it, eating the fish and then closing the lid and going back to its own tank.

Octopuses can recognize human faces too.

In one laboratory, a captive octopus disliked one of the staff. Every time the person went near the tank, the octopus squirted a jet of water at her.

Octopuses are clever and inquisitive creatures. Even so, many people like to eat them.

Do you want to eat an octopus?